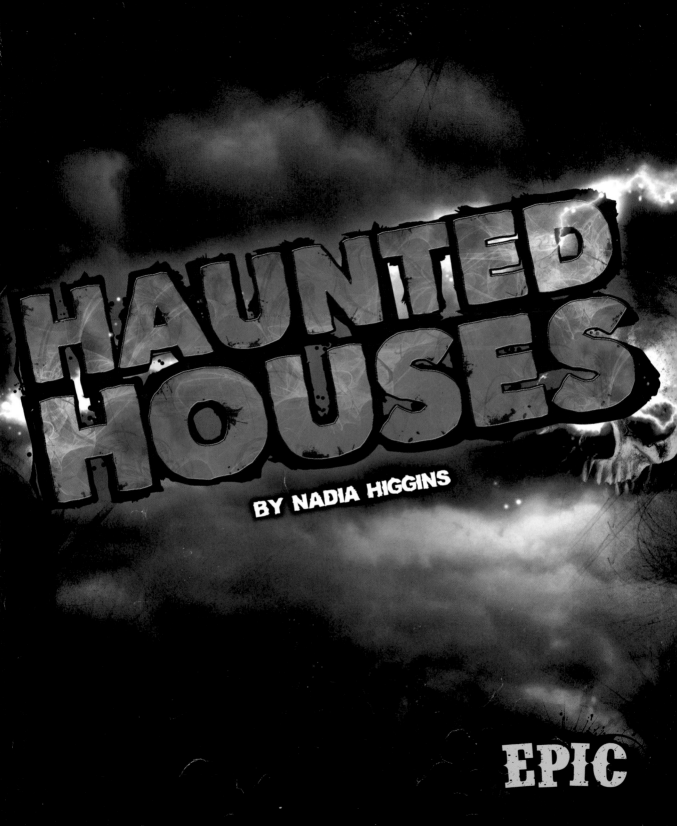

HAUNTED HOUSES

BY NADIA HIGGINS

EPIC

BELLWETHER MEDIA · MINNEAPOLIS, MN

EPIC BOOKS are no ordinary books. They burst with intense action, high-speed heroics, and shadows of the unknown. Are you ready for an Epic adventure?

This edition first published in 2014 by Bellwether Media, Inc.

No part of this publication may be reproduced in whole or in part without written permission of the publisher. For information regarding permission, write to Bellwether Media, Inc., Attention: Permissions Department, 5357 Penn Avenue South, Minneapolis, MN 55419.

Library of Congress Cataloging-in-Publication Data

Higgins, Nadia.
  Haunted Houses / by Nadia Higgins.
    pages cm. – (Epic : Unexplained Mysteries)
  Summary: "Engaging images accompany information about haunted houses. The combination of high-interest subject matter and light text is intended for students in grades 2 through 7"– Provided by publisher.
  Audience: Ages 7-12.
  Includes bibliographical references and index.
  ISBN 978-1-62617-105-3 (hardcover : alk. paper)
  1. Haunted houses–Juvenile literature. I. Title.
  BF1475.H54 2014
  133.1'22–dc23
                    2013038411

Text copyright © 2014 by Bellwether Media, Inc. EPIC and associated logos are trademarks and/or registered trademarks of Bellwether Media, Inc. SCHOLASTIC, CHILDREN'S PRESS, and associated logos are trademarks and/or registered trademarks of Scholastic Inc.

Designed by Jon Eppard.

Printed in the United States of America, North Mankato, MN.

TABLE OF CONTENTS

A FRIGHTFUL NIGHT

Hissssssssssss. A young girl sits up in bed. "Who's there?" she calls. She hears more whispers. Is it just the wind?

Suddenly, her door slams shut. Then a strange light glows in the mirror. The girl screams. Are ghosts haunting her house?

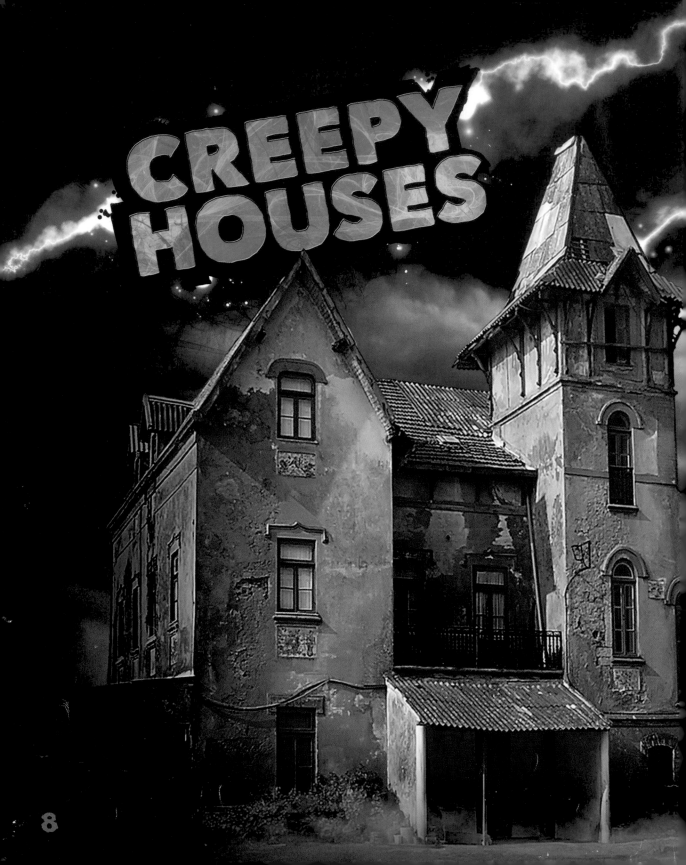

CREEPY HOUSES

People all over the world tell ghost stories. Many are about ghosts that haunt old houses. Often the houses become haunted after a **tragedy**.

MAKE YOURSELF AT HOME
Some people think the spirits of the dead stay at the places where they died.

Strange things happen in haunted houses. Doors creak open and slam shut on their own. Objects move across rooms. People even see ghosts or orbs.

SHOW ME A SIGN
Flickering lights, cold spots, and strange smells are also often reported in haunted houses.

One famous haunted house is in Amityville, New York. In the 1970s, the Lutz family lived in the house for only 28 days. The family left because evil things happened. They believed a demon was inside.

A DARK PAST
Six people were murdered in the house about a year before the Lutz family moved in.

13

ANYBODY HOME?

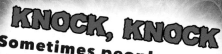

KNOCK, KNOCK

Sometimes people gather in a haunted house to talk to ghosts. The ghosts are believed to answer with knocks or whispers.

Paranormal investigators try to find proof that a house is haunted. They go inside with cameras and sound recorders. They also bring thermometers to follow cold spots.

15

Many believers do not need physical proof. They have experienced strange things firsthand. They claim there is no other explanation for what they saw or heard.

Skeptics argue that there are normal answers. Drafty windows can bring in cool air. Old wiring can make lights flicker. People might be seeing ghosts in their dreams.

HAUNTED HOUSES IN AMERICA

Franklin Castle
Cleveland, Ohio
In the 1800s, an entire family died at this old house. Today, people still hear the ghostly sounds of crying children.

Myrtles Plantation
St. Francisville, Louisiana
At this old slave house, the grand piano plays by itself. Sometimes it keeps playing one creepy chord!

The Whaley House
San Diego, California
Several men were hanged where this house stands. Visitors claim to see their ghosts. A ghost dog has been spotted, too.

The White House
Washington, D.C.
Even presidents say they have seen ghosts here. Abraham Lincoln is often spotted.

The Winchester House
San Jose, California
This 160-room house was worked on nonstop for 38 years. It has stairs and hallways that lead to dead ends. They were built to confuse spirits that haunted the owner!

The Winchester House

Franklin Castle

Myrtles Plantation

Old houses give many people the creeps. Is it because they are often run-down and empty? Or do ghosts roam around inside haunting them?

GLOSSARY

creak—to squeak slowly

demon—an evil spirit

drafty—cold because of the movement of cool air

firsthand—from personal experience

orbs—balls of light

paranormal—strange happenings that cannot be explained by natural causes

recorders—small devices that record sounds

run-down—in bad condition due to old age and poor care

skeptics—people who doubt the truth of something

tragedy—a horrible event that causes deep sadness

TO LEARN MORE

At the Library

Hennessy, B. G. *The Scary Places Map Book: Seven Terrifying Tours.* Somerville, Mass.: Candlewick, 2012.

Perish, Patrick. *Are Haunted Houses Real?* Mankato, Minn.: Amicus, 2014.

Von Finn, Denny. *Stanley Hotel.* Minneapolis, Minn.: Bellwether Media, 2014.

On the Web

Learning more about haunted houses is as easy as 1, 2, 3.

1. Go to www.factsurfer.com.

2. Enter "haunted houses" into the search box.

3. Click the "Surf" button and you will see a list of related Web sites.

With factsurfer.com, finding more information is just a click away.

INDEX